# ANGEL EYES

A COLLECTIVE MEMOIR OF CHILD SEXUAL ABUSE

BY

KATANDRA SHANEL JACKSON

Published by

FreedomInk Publishing

P O Box 161965

Atlanta Georgia 30321

Copyright © April 2012 by Katandra Shanel Jackson

All rights reserved. No part of this publication may be reproduced or transmitted in any form or by any means, electronic or mechanical, including photocopy, recording, or any information storage and retrieval system, without permission in writing from the copyright owner.

Cover design by Elaina Lee.
Page layout by FreedomInk Publishing.
Foreword by Dr. Darcova Triplett
Proofread by Donna Jean Bennett.
Computer generated images by Herman Taylor II

Final edit by Katandra Shanel Jackson.

Cover Model, Kaylee Ann Marie Meek

ISBN 978-0-985-1041-0-8

Printed in the United States of America

www.freedomink365.com

## PREFACE

Collected within these pages are statistics, related poetry, definitions, and the collective memoirs of several women ranging in age, personality, and overall family dynamics. The common thread that connects them to each other and other women of the world is the shame they've felt at the hands of child sexual abuse. Within these pages we stand up, speak out and claim the shame no more. No more hiding behind angel eyes. This pain is not ours alone. It belongs to a Nation. This is our story…

# ACKNOWLEDGEMENTS

Once again, acknowledging my ever supportive and patient family.

My tolerant children; Trevon, Kailyn, & Ashley, who let me take over the kitchen table thereby placing them in the living room in front of the television during meal times, which by the way, they never complain about.

My soul mate, Herman, who encourages me to create a space, any space away from the bustle of home life. The only available space, a filled-to-capacity laundry room which we've since reorganized and converted into an office. It's my own little space, a room of my own!

My mother for dreaming dreams, she saw the outcome before it began.

My sister in law, for prophesizing that which I was unsure of.

Family & Friends for believing in me.

Thanks and I love each of y'all.

## SPECIAL THANKS

Mr. and Mrs. Robert Collins of Bellville, Georgia

Dominic and Brandi Conger

Shannia and Sonya Lewis

Dr. Darcova Triplett

John and Michelle Mobley

Yolanda Clay Triplett

Trinette T'Shon Collier

Yvette Porter Moore

Nikita Jackson-Holmes

Tanja Robinson

LaVerne @ SWAG {Sisters With A Goal}

Nicholas 'Redd' Scott Sr. @ Redds Buttons

&

Herman Taylor II

In addition to these 'Special Angels of FreedomInk' I'd also like to acknowledge the gracious sponsors of the Angel Eyes Foundation. Thank you!

AN EXCEPTIONAL THANKS TO THE WOMEN WHO CAME FORWARD. THANKS FOR SHARING YOUR STORIES WITH ME AND THE WORLD. IN DOING SO YOU'VE STRENGTHENED YOURSELF AND GIVEN THE COURAGE TO ANOTHER TO SPEAK UP. THANK YOU.

# DEDICATION

I dedicate this book to the girls.

I dedicate this book to the children of South Africa where a pandemic has occurred. By popular belief and myth, men with HIV are attempting to rid themselves of the disease by having sex with virgins, babies & children.

I dedicate this book to the women who have made the miraculous transition of Victim to Survivor, those that shared their stories with me, with the world, and those that will find the courage within these pages to speak up and out against this cruelty.

An old African Proverb states "It takes a village to raise a child." We are all in this together. Let's protect our greatest resource. Without them there is no future…

I dedicate this book to the children of the world.

# ON THE OUTSIDE LOOKING IN

### A Foreword by Dr. Darcova Triplett

You look fine to me. Got your quality education, own your own business, big house and fancy car. I see you loving on your husband, laughing with your children and sashaying with your friends. You strut around here like you know you know you know you got it going on. On the outside looking in, it's the perfect picture. Your cover shouts, "YES I CAN!" You exude confidence and epitomize assertion. Your words are powerful and your endeavors are purposeful. The world is at your fingertips and you can do whatever… whenever.

But then you let me come a little closer. What's this I see? Invisible tears. Lingering fears. Incessant pain. Uncompromising shame. You allow me to walk in your shoes, just for a moment, and my senses are startled! I smell the putrid aroma in the air. I taste his acerbic juices. I feel your agony and anguish and animosity and abhorrence… I hear your prayers.

As I return your shoes and step back outside, I will forever carry a piece of you with me. And my perspective will never be the same.

## INTRODUCTION

We never know to whom we speak when true words are spoken. Because the audience is unknown we oftentimes keep these words to ourselves. Even worse than silence is truths untold! I have been instructed to come forward, out of the shadows and into the light.

A very long time ago, the man I loved and admired took innocence for granted. He abused his authority, shattered a life before it began, and broke a daughter's heart. It's hard to forgive and forget, even harder letting go. I am opening clenched fists and releasing this pain.

Signed,

    Stolen Innocence

# DISCLOSURE

I'm no med school graduate nor do I possess any degrees in the medical field. What I am though is a woman who has come undone at the hands of child sexual abuse. I have crawled through the typical victim phases. I have been diagnosed "off the record" as being borderline depressed and asked a million personal questions by obstetricians and gynecologists alike as to the extent of scar tissue in my vagina. I've been called names. I've been let down. I've been cheated on, due in part to low self-esteem. I've been left alone, unable to trust, keeping at arms distant every man attempting to emotionally get close. I've been suicidal, entertaining morbid thoughts. I've been angry. I've been afraid. I've been martyred, molested, and maimed. But here I stand, out of the shadows and into the light. I am 'The Survivor'.

\*Names have been altered to protect the identities of parties involved, and to safeguard the privacy of the women whose stories lie within these pages.

*"...there's a very old soul that dwells inside this shell. Her body has known much pain and her eyes have bear witness to malice at such a sweet age..."*

There are many types of sexual abuse. Of them, those that consummate in forced sexual acts are generally referred to as rape.

# RAPE

The crime of forcing a person to submit to sexual intercourse; seizing and carrying off by force; violating.

## STATISTICALLY SPEAKING

In 2002, 150 million girls under the age of 18 were the victim of sexual abuse. 1 in 4 women will be sexually abused before their 18th birthday.

## THE MOST COMMON TYPES OF SEXUAL ABUSE

Just as the faces of its victims, the types of Sexual Abuse are many. The most common are inflicted by those we know, and usually take place in the home of the victim or some other familiar place.

- Acquaintance Rape where forced sex is imposed by a friend or acquaintance.

- Partner Rape which occurs between partners, married or not, when the act is nonconsensual.

- Stranger Rape happens less often, the abuser is unknown to the victim.

Yes, them too. Common or not, most forms of Rape target women, although there are cases where males are the victim.

## THE ALMOST PERFECT CRIME

Because statistics are ever changing, it's difficult to project an exact estimate of those who have been sexually abused. Although, most studies show that only 40% of sexual abuse cases are ever reported to the police, more than ½ never speak up.

**DEAD SILENCE**

Nary a witness
verbal threats hissed
physical force
vicious & venomous
violence
raped into silence.

Because so few women ever report these heinous acts, the perpetrator goes unpunished. Unpaid consequences subsequently open the window to a world of repeat offense, casting a much larger web. In its wake a new batch of victims are left broken and unspoken. As the cycle continues rape truly does mimic the perfect crime. Worse still are the victims who are often left questioning more than the assault itself.

# RECIDIVISM

A tendency to lapse into a previous pattern or behavior.

FYI: In the prison population, those most likely to return have already been convicted of sex crimes.

*Why did this happen to me?*

*What did I do to deserve this?*

*Will anyone believe me?*

*Is this my fault?*

*What will others think?*

*Will I be harmed, or worse killed for speaking up?*

Afraid of the answers to these questions victims remain silent, some for a short while, others for a lifetime. It is in this silence that they feel as if their lives have been forever shattered.

### MORNING COMES

Broken body. Shattered
Like the wings of a wounded bird
Flightless. Furthermore a refusal to sing
Unable to see the rays of sun
peeking through the storm
She doesn't yet know
that morning comes.

You are not alone. Statistics and studies have calculated that a woman is sexually assaulted every 2 minutes in the United States alone. This is more than 600 women per day.

**SOLITUDE**

**S**ilent tears fall down the face

**O**f the one who

**L**ives

**I**n pain… she

**T**ries to hide the hurt she feels

**U**nderneath unreal smiles… and all the while she is

**D**ying for the world to understand the

**E**pitome of who she is

Because rape is a national crisis, it does not target any one specific group. The face of Predator and Prey are many. Although, there is usually one uncommonality.

The Predator: (usually) Male          The Prey: (usually) Female

TWO NONDISCRIMINATE DEPICTIONS OF PREDATOR AND PREY ALIKE

Various ethnicities

Undefined financial boundaries

Although usually male, the perpetrator can be either gender

Although usually female, the victim can be either gender

Insignificant educational backgrounds

Environmental factors don't matter

With such a wide range of demographics it's no wonder that child sexual abuse is a separate issue altogether.

**IN THE BEGINNING THERE WAS INNOCENCE...**

**EASY...**

Small

Weak & Frail

What better victim

than a

Child?

Child sexual abuse may be suspected to make up the largest percentage of under-reported and non-filed crime. This twisted phenomenon is often a mental game of cat and mouse.

# The Hunter

# V/s

# The Hunted

## …PREY

Waiting. Watching

Watching. Waiting

The even steady breaths

Are breathed quiet and calmly

A sweet aroma fills the air

The smell of her grows stronger as he nears

Intoxicated he becomes as he waits

And when she least expects, he dangles the bait

A father's love and a family whole

Strength, security, and a bond of old

A father's wishes turned into a lover's kisses

And the world which was once safe and snug

Disappeared with a father's love

**…AND THEN INNOCENCE WAS NO MORE!**

The most commonly, unreported acts of rape are committed against those too immature to defend themselves mentally, physically, and emotionally. They are the young & innocent.

According to the United Nations Convention on the Rights of the Child, a child is any human being below the age of eighteen years.

## INEXCUSED CRUELTY

As are many, I too am fascinated with psychology. Why people act a certain way, what makes us tick, varying personalities, our alikes and differences. The branch of psychology that intrigues me the most is that which relates to children. Such a delight to watch unfold all the phases and stages. Amongst those stages is sexual exploration which is a normal part of childhood, beginning in infancy, lasting throughout adolescence and puberty, and bleeding over into puberty. This is a process that enables us to lead productive lives on a reproductive level. What then if this natural order of things is disturbed? What if the balance is affected by outside factors?

To be raped at such a critical time in one's life can be detrimental in later years, emotionally & mentally. Which brings me back to psychology, especially that of the mind. It perplexes me, but I'm certain that the psyche of the rapist is not well. Such cruelty towards children is something I doubt society as a whole will ever understand. Child sexual abuse as with rape in general, is and always will be an inexcused cruelty.

Rape is a sick and twisted disease, infecting and affecting a nation. Of any nature, sexual abuse is a crime. When any sexual activity toward children comes into play one tends to wonder what type of pleasure is being gained?

# SADISM

The association of sexual gratification with infliction of pain on others.

THE WHO, WHAT, WHEN, WHERE, WHY OF CHILD SEXUAL ABUSE

Who: The victim, usually female, any age with a dramatic increase in those between the ages of 10-14.

What: any sexual activity perpetrated against a child by threat, force, intimidation, or manipulation, abusing the relationship of power and authority that adults have over children.

When: A crime of this nature can happen at any time although meal time hours seem common.

Where: Usually occurs in a familiar place, i.e. the child's home.

Why: A lot of factors seem to play a part in this phenomenon but no one is truly certain why.

## THE CYCLE

Prey

Weak

Frail

Afraid

Lost

Silenced

Abused

Misused

Misunderstood

Girl

Woman

Sister

Friend

Cousin

Mother

Daughter

Victim

Survivor

## WHAT'S DONE IS DONE

What yall think? Tellin' is easy? What if my mama ain't believing my daddy could look at me with the same eyes he look at her? What if she don' care cause he purr er'time he call me 'SweetThang'. What if he hug'n on me all da time tawkin' bout how i'ma make some boy happy. But befo' that happen, he might as well teach me what bein' a woman bout. Make me do stuff to him in the day that I can't scape at night. And the teachin' seem like it ain't gon eva end. A day turn into years.

Husband think I don't love him. I gets the creeps under my skin er'time he touch on me. Purrs he love me all the time. I believe him in my heart but I can't help how I feel. Still ain't told him bout that god awful stuff that happened to me so long ago. Not sho it matter much now. What he gon' think? Probably same thang my mama woulda thought. She loved me too. Guess I didn't love myself huh?

Sincerely,

Too Late Now

## WHY

Why should these pains cause sleepless nights and dreaded days? Why should we be afraid? Why do we feel the need to protect someone other than ourselves? Why don't we tell? Why do we allow the pain of the sharp dull blade to persist? Why do we doubt our own existence? Why must we feel unworthy of a clean slate? Why not speak up and out? When will our day break?

# END THE CYCLE...

# BREAK THE CHAIN!

### A FAMILY MATTER, A PRIVATE AFFAIR, OR A PUBLIC SHAME?

Younger children are usually too afraid to disclose the abuse and older children feel a need to uphold the family name. A family matter becomes a private affair, and it in turn becomes a public shame. Forced to live a lie, these secrets ruin the lives of so many. Only the strong survive. Determined not to be a victim of childhood circumstances... finally unafraid of the shame, we speak up & out against the homes, neighborhoods, and communities that were entrusted with our lives. It's time the world knew our pain does indeed exist. These horrific tales are real. We were victimized but we have chosen to SURVIVE!

A bond of old, a relationship that is forged of familial ties, spectacular; it is thought to withstand time itself. For it is he that sets the standard of each encounter thereafter. What daughter doesn't on some level look for her father in the capable hands of her future husband? What if that bond is violated and the ties are severed? What if the unthinkable happens…?

**FATHERS & DAUGHTERS: A TALE OF INCEST**

The most common type of child sexual abuse is Incest, especially that between father & daughter.

# INCEST

Any sexual activity between individuals so closely related that marriage is prohibited. Incest involving a child is a form of child sexual abuse.

## DADDY'S PRINCESS

I'm going to do my best to recall what memory, heart, and body has tried so hard to forget. Just yesterday I got sick to my stomach from the mere thought of thinking about…. I was at the library standing between the rows of books, the stacks of volumes, the smell of paper and cedar strong in my nostril. I picked up a book and began reading. Each of us has a story to tell, and each is as different as we, still it goes without saying that all things in the universe are connected. As I read a testimony of another's pain at the hands of child sexual abuse, old wounds opened and scars revealed themselves. My heart was racing and I could feel my body and psyche react to a story that was dauntingly similar to my own. With a vengeful conscious I dismissed each thought and every emotion that stemmed from limbs. Shaking the ill that came flooding back, I cleared my head and tried to remember where I was. Gathering all senses I made a beeline for the exit. Fresh air in my nostrils and the stench of yesteryears not far behind I sped home as if to leave it in its wake. Safely within the confines of home I press my back against the door, warding off any evil that dare enter. Calming, I can feel the love emitting from these walls. I knew this day would come. The day I would have to face my past and stop running. Uncomfortably I prepared to open myself to the hurts that had inadvertently changed the course of my life. And as hurtful as I knew it would be, I welcomed every sound, smell and painful detail.

I close my eyes, I breathe, I remember. The place I sit is no longer familiar…

He had never been a part of my life! Well not the way a father is should be. But I suppose two are to blame for that happenstance. Still over the years

I had retained enough memories of him, bits and pieces from those around me and from the occasional, past encounters. Alongside a younger sibling, I was raised by a mother who was on-again off-again single. 'Privileged' to spend summers near him, mostly with his parents, my grandparents. He already had a family and I had long since been disincluded. Two younger siblings I had been deprived the honor of being a 'big sister' to and a stepmother that hated me! Perhaps that judgment is harsh, but even at a very young age I knew that was a mere technicality, one that she would just as soon not acknowledge. Odd how she indirectly plays a major part in this story.

I remember it like it was yesterday, the papers my mother signed that unfortunate day. Papers I was later told were thought to be temporary guardianship forms, should any medical issues arise. I was glad that I had successfully completed 5th grade and was looking forward to my vacation. Still, it was odd for 'her' to be there, picking up the package. It was the summer of 1990. The car ride across several states was agonizing if not uneventful. We were fast approaching and I would soon be face to face with the man who was my father.

## THAT FIRST ENCOUNTER

I can remember thinking "He's so big! So this is my daddy." I had seen him before but this was the first time I really 'saw' him. A glimpse here, a moment there, all those pieces of him I had stored away for this day. Finally, it was upon me. Nice was hardly the correct word to describe one so rugged. He was downright scary to a girl of 10. Here he was this big, burly man with menacing scowl. No one else seemed intimidated by him; I assumed it was his way. He was in the den, the room that would be later converted into my very own bedroom. He didn't hug me, despite the years that had passed since we had seen each other last. I can remember my mother watching the news praying he was okay while across seas, fighting in a war the rest of us cared less about. And me thinking, what's all the fuss about? He doesn't love her or me, so why love him? Why care? But deep down, secretly, I did. The idea of being daddy's girl was as enticing as a bowl of candy… simply sweet. And even though I didn't know him, I wanted that! He was the one thing missing in my single parent life. I wanted him to be my daddy.

Funny thing about children, they have a 6th sense the rest of the world has forgotten…

His wife was withdrawn. She always had this very cold look in her eyes when she looked at me, as if someone prepared her soup with spoiled milk. I was there upsetting the balance within the walls of her happy home. It was a look I learned to interpret as dislike for my mother and the life my father had before her. I really, really loved the idea of being a big sister again, 2 younger brothers came with this new family. Not to mention my grandparents lived close by. There was also a gang of cousins, aunts, and uncles. I could dismiss a few looks for the duration of a summer for the sake of family. My vacation began and unfolded in a typical manner I suppose. It was at summer's end that my life took an unexpected turn. The sweetness of summer faded, my Grandfather passed away, and my world died with him. They say suppressed memory is a coping mechanism. That the mind forgets what it forgets on purpose, shutting off painful memories so that the body can continue to function. But even with memories ½ forgotten, one thing remains effervescently clear…

THE FIRST TIME

We left the family behind at my grandmother's house. Nothing assuming about dad and daughter making a trip to the store, right? Instead of pulling into the well-lit, car filled parking lot; he parked his truck behind a dark, secluded building. An old warehouse or abandoned school? The family was close because I can remember only riding for a few short minutes. He turned the truck off and told me to take off my seatbelt and get into the backseat. I never questioned him prior to this moment, he was my father and all words were spoken with authority. I obeyed. I had to crawl over the front seat to do so. Gangly limbs must have been so awkward then. He turned around and in a voice not his own, told me to take off my clothes. Out of fear, I obliged again, this time with much trepidation. Then he got out, opened the back door, and slid into the seat beside me. In the dark, I could hear the unzipping of his pants overpowered only by the sound of his breathing which was not loud enough to drown out my fear. I can still remember the sound, the feel of my heart beating in my ears, in my throat. I could feel him struggle in the seat as he pulled his pants down, then the warmth of his flesh as legs touched and the coldness of his hands at my shoulders commanding me to lie down. I had this overwhelming feeling in my gut that this was not right. Ashamed, I covered the beginning development of an undeveloped body, arms across chest, legs together bent, and knees tight against each other. A futile attempt to protect my fleeting innocence…

*Your strength is what makes you Beautiful…*

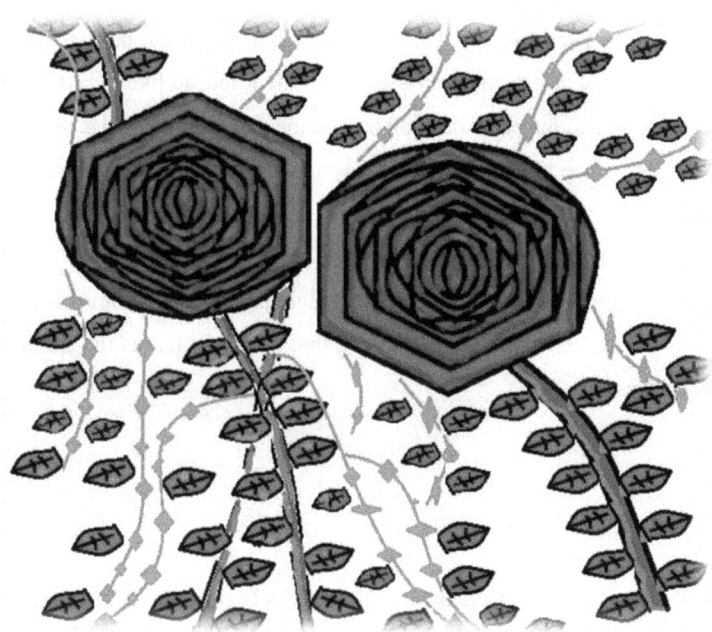

*No one can take that away from you!*

Fingers as cold as ice and as unforgiving as hell pried knees apart with a vice like grip. The mere hint of moonlight shone through the windows and I could see the look in his eyes, a look of lust and hate all at once. It was a look I was too young to understand then, but it was not one of fatherly love and admiration. As I looked into his eyes, a daughter's pleads went unheeded. This man was no longer my father. The weight of his body was unreal as he positioned himself over me, placing himself between my knees. As he penetrated me, I never made a sound. I was too afraid, too embarrassed. I felt like I had let him take the most private part of me. I felt dirty. When he was done he kissed me on the forehead like everything was ok. As he pulled his pants back on he told me that if I ever told anyone that I would never see my mother again. My mind was blank. I don't recall any thoughts after that first time. I don't recall getting dressed, I don't recall going back to my grandmother's to pick up the family, I don't recall going home. I just remember lying in bed that night praying that it never happened again, and at the same time pretending that it hadn't. It was the summer of 1991, I was 11.

A DAUGHTER'S LOVE

The next time it happened was a few weeks later, in the bedroom that had been given to me as a present. It was the same room he was in during that first encounter at summer's start, the same room I was allowed to paint however a little girl's heart so desired… hot pink and black, my favorite colors. Now I lay in this room with my back pressed hard against the ugly brown carpet as he continued to take for granted a daughter's love. I can remember thinking, 'she' must know. Five steps from the room where my stepmother lay, probably awake. I wished she would die. He would visit my room so often on his way to work in the mornings, he would tell me to sleep without panties on. Most mornings I pretend to be asleep when he entered my bedroom. He would pick me up out of bed, lay me on the floor, and heist my gown. Then the touching. His fingers inside of me. He would openly moan as I winced in pain as those sausage like fingers plundered and probed, further shaming me.

After those first few times he became gentle. Always baby talking me, caressing me, smoothing my hair, and touching my skin. It was like he was willing me to love him after the hurt he had done and the nightmares he had unleashed… and I did. He was my daddy. And despite the hurt he could do no wrong. I had lived the better part of my childhood without him and now that he was in my life I wanted to be loved by him. I wanted him to be my daddy, still. His wife always seemed to be mad or pissed off at something, mainly me. And my daddy would swoop in and save me. Sheltering me, giving me extra love where a stepmothers affections fell short for a little girl, rides and alone time without little brothers in tow, extra treats, extra attention, ice cream outings, movies and popcorn. All of this done with fatherly intent and love, nothing foul, these were good days. I was his special girl, and when he wasn't violating me I loved him most. Not every day was bad!

Too many firsts. How sad…

The first time my breasts were touched. The first time a man would put his face between my legs to taste me. The first man I would perform oral sex on… him! Sometimes he would make me kiss him 'there'. Telling me the correct way to hold my mouth wide open so that I didn't bite him, the proper way to suck and lick and hold 'him' while he thrust, gagging me. I remember this one time when the family left for a weekend and as usual they left me behind like an old ragdoll. That first day alone, he put me on a pedestal. I wasn't his princess. I was Queen for a day! Daddy all to myself without 'her' shooting daggers, I was beginning to dislike her and he seemed to bask in the mutual hate. The daytime was sweet for daddy's little girl, but nightfall came all too quick. He washed me in the shower and lay me in their bed on her side. He told me he was "making love" to me and that this was how he loved me. He smoothed my hair and kissed my breasts. There had been moments of thrill when my body felt really good because of what he was doing to me, but I would block those feelings with thoughts of hate. But for some reason this night, I couldn't. My mind felt weak as my body spasmed in the place where his tongue was. Later I would learn that what I had experienced was my first orgasm. It felt good, but I knew it wasn't right. After that weekend, he made me seek out his 'love'.

What had spanned the course of months with weekly intervals became habitual, daily. Then nothing. And like a junkie addicted to drugs, I experienced withdrawals from his emotional and physical detachment. He didn't even fill the role of father. He told me to let him know when I wanted his 'love'. This was hard to do but I felt like I was missing something. So I did. He made me tell him I wanted him. Then my heart softened. I felt sorry for him. Why did he have to be married to such a bitter woman, she always seemed so cold and withdrawn. I felt like I was the only one that loved him.

Victims of long-term rape have been known to develop Stockholm syndrome.

# Stockholm Syndrome

A phenomenon in which a hostage begins to identify with and grow sympathetic to his or her captor.

This 'secret' between father and daughter continued for 2 years.

The following events transpired in a chaotic whir. My life was tipping, tilting, at a vertical slant. Intentionally & increasingly to the point it was upside down. Throughout it all, I never spoke a word of it. ½ out of fear… ½ out of love… until I found escape from it all within the pages of my very 1st diary. I don't think she, my stepmother, intended for it to be a refuge, but it became that just the same. Sharing secrets buried in that diary is the only thing that saved me. My then bestfriend had the courage I did not to speak up. She read my words and in turn became my voice. She told her parents what I had shared with her. Police came to my father's home and removed me. The disillusion of daydreams ended but the nightmares remained.

NIGHTMARES HAUNT ME STILL

Twenty years later I'm still affected by this traumatic event that has in its own way redefined certain aspects of my life. My uneasiness when it comes to trusting men, my inability to orgasm, a memory that is short lived and always failing, and a forever nagging fear that history will repeat itself through my own daughters. For this I hated him. For a very long time, I hated him for what he had done to me, how he made me feel, how he had ultimately 'loved' me. I hated him for not being a Father...

I have since attempted to reconnect with my father since having children of my own. Revisiting a place of pain, needing closure and confirmation, answers as to why and the reassurance that what happened was not my fault. The apologies that should have not been required had a daughter been allowed to be a little girl, came too many years too late. The damage has been done. Body, mind, spirit, and soul were left like a pile of broken glass and I know I'll be picking up the pieces forever. I still have a long way to go before reaching 'HAPPILY EVER AFTER'.

Sincerely,

    Fathers Like Fairytales Don't Exist...

## UNCONVENTIONAL

Unconventional the relationship between Dad & Daughter

When he alone neglects the role of father

Touches child in manner one would a Lover

No wonder she can't love another

Studies suggest that fathers may have a considerable impact on their daughter's self-esteem and he may greatly influence her choice of romantic partners. (Scheffler and Naus, 1999)

## LOST

I was sexually abused as a child, victimized on a weekly basis, on a daily basis to the point of disturbia. Childhood was no longer normal. Adulthood abnormal too, but that's a different story. Everyday life since has been an ongoing struggle just to stay afloat. An overwhelming feeling like the walls are closing in, claustrophobic. I suppose I felt that's what drowning must be like. Lost, I return to what has been drilled in me. Instilled in me. It's the only thing that I for certain know. His voice, his touch, his 'love'.

Signed,

Desperately attempting to navigate this Sea called Life

Prince's Diamonds and Pearls loud in my ears, the taste of burnt cabbage scorched against my tongue, sketches of the nude form, images and sounds burned into my mind from the exposure of explicit, pornographic scenes will forever be mine…

## RECALLING A MEMORY

1/2 Asleep

Hearing the door creak

Open

Then close

Feeling him watching me

Pretending to be asleep

Feeling his hands on me

Lifting my juvenile night gown

Tugging at my panties

Pulling them down

Past my ankles

The faint sound of them

Hit the floor

The heat of his body

Getting

Closer

Hot, harsh, hateful breaths

Roughness, wetness

Tongue licking

Inner most private parts

Fingers probing me

Digging me

Forcing the girl in me

To

Die
Shaming the woman
Not yet ready to live
A horrific spasm
Body limp
Senses numb
Hands snatch legs apart
What is the worst part?
The flesh I can feel ripping
Later told
"Scar tissue"
The heavy panting in my ear
The
"I love you baby girl, touch me here."

Or

The blackness drawing near
In and out of consciousness
Removing mind
Leaving body behind
A horrific spasm
The weight of his body
Unforgiving
On mine
With eyes still closed
Afraid to look
He's sitting me up
Tells me to
"Wake up
get out of bed
then

down on the floor"
That ugly brown carpet
Scratches my knees
And I can feel every
Breath I Breathe
And I can see every inch of him
Flesh
Skin
Blood of my own
Lifts my chin
Tells me to
"Open your mouth."
Then puts it in
One hand at my face
Squeezing
"Don't bite, open wide."
One hand on my head
Pulling me close
Closer
Suffocating me
Choking me
Then again
Horrific spasm
I can feel his thumb at my throat
And cream fill my mouth
"Swallow!"
I feel sick
Lost. Afraid. Confused
He looks down at me
Mockingly lovingly
Watching me sit

In a pool of my own
Shame and misery
Caresses me
Puts my panties back on
Helps me back into bed
Pulls the covers up
Whispers
"Daddy loves you."
Kisses me on the forehead
But his little girl is already dead.

## A PLAGUE UPON OUR NATION

Funny how I love him still. Why is this? Does this make me insane? Should I hate one that will forever be a part of my life? Why do I love him? Why don't I hate him when I think that I should and I'm certain the rest of the world feels the same. Some days I believe that we both were the victims. Perhaps his mind was ill affected by the war he took part in and the man that returned that summer was not my Father. Or what if he experienced firsthand the nightmare which he in turn inflicted? Had my father been sexually abused and manipulated as a child? Is this a genetic disease that has passed down through the generations? Will this disease reroute prewired neurons in the brains of those still in the womb? Will we inevitably birth a generation of sexually confused individuals who have become desensitized by adaptation? Will the cycle repeat itself on a default or technicality? What can we do to rid our Nation of this Plague?

The confusion of sex as love can lead to promiscuity, as one attempts over and over again with no luck to find that which seems to never remember her name.

-The whole town

calls me a whore

A loved one raped me

at the tender age of four.

Therapist said

it's how I show love.

People hear my name,

but 'whore' is all

they think of...

Over exposure to explicit material could possibly trigger in the mind of the abused an addictive behavior.

...and the authority that was placed in those hands was abused...

## FORGOTTEN

When I was 8 my mom left my dad whom I loved dearly, taking me with her. We moved away to a new town. She met someone new. He seemed like a good man, at least that's what I thought. She went out a lot, my mother. He seemed cool with it which I didn't understand but would soon find out why. One particular night she was getting ready to go out I begged her to stay with me. I was scared. My brothers were gone and I felt like everybody was leaving me. So she says, "*Miles is here, you don't have to be afraid. I'll be back in a little while." He tried to calm me down by saying, "We're going to have fun, don't worry." As soon as my mom left and the door was closed, he came up behind me. I was just standing there with my back turned to the house. My mom's boyfriend put his hand on my shoulder and turns me around and demands me to kiss him. I was thinking a kiss on the cheek, I'm only 8. What do I know about kissing? So I kiss him on the cheek. He laughs and says he wants a 'real kiss'. I'm totally confused, so I just stand there. He grabs me and says "I'm bout to teach you how to kiss like a woman." The next thing I know his tongue is in my mouth. It was the most disgusting thing ever. After he stopped I began spitting, I guess that made him mad because the next thing I know I was being drug down the hall to my room. He slung me in there, turned off the light, and shut my door. I thought I was just in trouble or something. I could hear him walking through the house, turning off lights and cussing, but I didn't think anything of it. A couple of minutes later he's back in my room turning on the light and telling me to take off my clothes, that if I didn't he was going to whip me. Scared to death, I did as I was told. He just stood there looking at me, at what I don't know. At 8 I didn't have much of a body. So he starts smiling and touching on me. Without reliving word for word, let's just say he had his way with little ol' me. He said that if I ever told anyone he would kill my momma. So I never said anything. That day I was turned into a girl nobody knew or understood. I became quiet and standoffish and I secretly blamed my mom for not protecting me. Making matters worse, the day it happened was my birthday. And it sucks because now i'm reminded every year on what is supposed to be a joyous day, of the day I was forgotten.

Signed,

   Left Behind

# RUNAWAY

I attempted to run away once! At least I think I did. Now that I think back on it, perhaps it was a figmented recollection of my imagination. But I'm certain I tried to escape the sadness. Maybe it was a vividly seen daydream to take mind away from body while my father reached his climax, came inside of me, and then grew limp. The weight of his body unforgiving, as breaths grew short under the pressure of crushed ribs. I contemplated suicide once! At least I think I did. Now what would that have solved? The end of my pain? What of that my mother would surely endure? What of the pain and nightmares awaiting his nieces, my cousins? I was too afraid to speak up, too afraid to leave the hurt and pain. So even though my body stayed, my mind ran away.

Sincerely,

Longing to Be Free of the Memories That Continue to Trouble Me


# AWAY

Close my eyes. Feel the wind in my hair. The sand beneath my feet.
Never mind the rocks and shells that cut and make toes bleed.
Forgetting all senses. Leaving shoes behind
Body aching. Mind numb

as I run

Close my eyes. Feel the wind beneath my wings. High. High. Higher still.
So as not to feel the pain as it invades body and tries to rape mind.
Forgetting all senses. Leaving cares behind

## DECEPTION

Hoodwinked

Bamboozled

Led amuck

Mind manipulated

Body stuck

Cunning words

Naive girl led astray

Little did she know

The price she'd pay…

## PUPPY LOVE

I was 14. It was a couple of weeks before my birthday. I was at the store when I saw him, this handsome guy I had seen a time or two in the past. We never spoke. He said hello and I just smiled. I noticed he was significantly older than me, later I found out he was 16 years older than me... YIKES!! So long story short, while I was at the store it began to rain and the handsome stranger asked if I needed a ride. That ride was the beginning of the end of the young, innocent *Beth Ann that I really didn't have time to know very well. We talked. His words took control of my immature mind and I became 'his'. I soon found myself running behind his every breath. I spent the remainder of my teenage years controlled by him. It was something about his words that just took a hold of me so tight that I realized I wasn't my own person. I was 'his'. At the age of 17, I wanted it to end because I found out he was cheating. But when I tried to leave he wouldn't let me. It was the 1st worst night of my life. All I can remember is him slapping me and a gun to the side of my head with his words echoing in my ears, "You are mine!" I couldn't believe I was in this place. It wasn't over. I stayed out of fear.

I became pregnant and it was hard for me to be happy about becoming a mother because I felt trapped for life. I was 5 months pregnant when the 2nd worst day of my life happened. I came home from work to find 'him' in bed with another woman. I left the house and just rode around until I gathered my senses. When I got back he was waiting. I told 'him' I was leaving and he told me I wasn't. He locked me in a room and said I wasn't giving 'his' love away. When he tried to kiss me I looked away, so he told me to kiss his dick. He forced me to give him oral sex and then he raped me. I stayed in that room for 3 days. All 3 days he forced me to do those things. Finally he let me out. I was terrified to leave.

The abuse continued for two more years. The last straw, sex against my will, the final rape is what finally gave me the courage to leave. He raped me with no remorse in front of our son who was just a baby then, but it absolutely killed me inside. After that I left. I was too afraid to stay. I ran like hell. That was the best day of my life.

Sincerely,

    Heartbroken

Child Sexual Abuse includes but is not limited to the following actions: Touching and fondling of the breast and private parts, penetration of any type, digitally fingering, the introduction of any foreign object, sodomy, exhibitionism, masturbation, oral to genital contact, rape, incest, making a child watch pornography or any sexual act, showing of the genitals to a child, any indecent exposure, asking a child to touch their own private parts while watching and viewing the child's genitals without physical contact, having the child touch the private parts of the offender and introducing inappropriate material of a sexual nature, for example, showing nude photographs.

Satisfaction, enjoyment, pleasure, delight… by any means necessary.

# MOLEST

To subject to unwanted or improper sexual activity.

Sexual abuse is not just physical...

... It is however, a struggle for power. To be in control of another's body, mind, feelings, emotions, and actions is something that is sometimes too great for the offender to resist. Using to their advantage the role and position in the life of the victim. Taking for granted the authority that has been placed in trusted hands. The abuser seeks gratification by any means necessary. Penetration of the body is not always the goal. In this hunt for power it seems penetration of the mind is more enticing. The reward? Sexual stimulation. This is achieved in many ways...

## **TOUCHED**

I was about 4 or 5 years old... a long time ago, but I've always had a good memory, and I can remember it like it was yesterday...

My mom was never a party goer, but on this particular occasion her and her bestfriend Joni said they were going out. So my mom dropped me and my brother off at *Joni's house. Her husband was going to babysit me and my brother and his own two sons. I don't remember what happened during the day... but I remember that dreadful night. It was late and the boys had made pallets on the floor and I lay on the sofa. Through all of my childhood sleepovers, I was always last to fall asleep. So of course the boys lay asleep on the floor, and I was awake on the sofa still watching television. From down the dark hallway I heard, "psss psss'" I looked up and saw 'him' motioning with his finger for me to come. Eager to see what he wanted, I got up and followed 'him' where he lead me which was into the bathroom. Once in the bathroom, he unbuttoned my pants and pulled them down. Then he picked me up and sat me on top of the bathroom counter. He then unzipped his pants and began to stroke his penis up and down my private. I then said, "I want my pants back on." Then he whispered, "I'm not going to hurt you" and continued. The next memory I have is of him having me lay down on the sofa with my pants down while he just lay on top of me with his pants down. Then after a while he pulled my pants back up, buttoned them… and that was it. As far as I can recall this was a single incident. I always felt like what he did was wrong. I hadn't even started school yet… but I knew that it was a 'bad thing'. Then when I started sex education classes in elementary school, the conversations on 'good touch/bad touch' always made me feel uncomfortable. I can remember seeing a small padlock somewhere at home. I thought. "What if I could put that on my zipper every time we go over to Joni's and my momma keeps the key. Then when I go back home, she can unlock it and take it off." I was just a little girl, and in my mind, that padlock would solve my problem.

I grew up not mentioning it for a long time. My chest felt like there was this knot tied tight in it. Every time my mom would tuck me into bed at night, it was on the tip of my tongue to tell her about that night some 8 years ago. In my head I would be saying, "Okay I'm going to tell her tonight," then when she pulled the covers up on me inside my head I would be saying "Tell her now, tell her now!" But the words just wouldn't come out. I went through that mental torture every time she would tuck me in… for years. I would even say, "Momma come put me in the bed." thinking I finally had the courage to spill the beans. But every time I waited, she kissed my cheek, turned off the light, and shut the door. I would lay in the dark feeling that knot getting tighter and tighter, bigger and bigger. Then when I was around 12 years old, she tucked me in and this force came out of nowhere and made me open my mouth and say, "Momma, I got something to tell you." I told her everything, the whole story that had been beating my spirits down for the past 8 years. She looked into my eyes with sorrow. Pretty much at a loss for words, she asked "Did he put it inside you or just touch you with it?" I said,

"Just touched." Then she mumbled an okay and shut the door leaving me in the dark alone. I may have been alone in the dark, but I felt a huge sense of relief that put the biggest grin on my face. For once in 8 years, I could go to sleep peacefully. I could literally feel that knot unravel. I finally felt free.

The next day my mom told me that I was gonna have to tell *Joni everything I had told her the night before. We all went to the park and sat down on the benches. Then my mom looked at *Joni and said "*Heather has something to tell you." I looked at *Joni and clammed up. She looked alarmed and said softly, "What is it?" Then I took a deep breath and retold the horrid story once again. After I finished, she looked at me and said, "Why didn't you say anything?" I shrugged my shoulders then my mom said, "Okay you can go." I ran off to play with my brother and god brothers.

My mom was sadder than ever (but she didn't let it show) and I was happier than ever. I never heard anyone speak of it until one day my god brothers were over at our house. My brother asked, "Why don't we ever go to y'alls house anymore?" Then one of my god brothers said "Because of what daddy did to *Heather." I froze in place for a few seconds and I felt a flash of guilt. It went away when the boys carried on playing. A few years after that I walked in on my mom talking on the phone with *Joni, she was saying, "I know she remembers. I don't know what to do." Then she started crying. I knew she was talking about me, but I just pretended like I wasn't listening. Never a spoken word again. No charges were pressed, no break up with *Joni and her husband, no more talking about it, but no more knots in my chest.

This has affected me slightly throughout my life. I can remember sitting in the backseat with my brother and god brothers and I would always scoot away from them. I wanted a space between them and me but squashed in a backseat with boys made that near impossible. So I would just deal with it. My brother would always want to sleep in the bed with his big sister. I put the boy through pure hell! I would say in my sternest voice, "Scoot over!" he would move away from me and then I would say, "Scoot over some more." Then I would reach my arm over him and if I felt any space at all between him and the edge of the bed I would make him scoot some more. I wasn't satisfied until he was darn near falling off the edge of the bed. He would suffer through that and still want to sleep with his big sister. My sex life has been affected somewhat as well. Whenever a man would be on top, I sometimes would get this feeling of disgust. Sex pretty much hasn't ever been a pleasure for me. I even thought of being asexual, which is being in a relationship with someone and sex isn't involved. Well it's hard to find a guy like that. But I realize that being asexual isn't natural and maybe I needed to get over it. Just recently I learned that if I had a drink before sex, it would calm my mind. It would stop all the thoughts.

Then the birth of my own sons… I feel uncomfortable being touched by the oldest. Not all the time though, just every once in a while. He is very touchy with me because he's truly a momma's boy. Sadly, I often push him away. I'm not sure if this is related or not because I don't feel that way with my youngest son. He can cuddle with me and I feel motherly. But with my oldest son, it feels uncomfortable at times. He realizes this and I think it makes him feel neglected. I am trying to get over this, but I wish I didn't feel like that from the beginning. Maybe I feel like that with the baby boy because I look at him as being 'the baby' and the oldest as being 'grown'… still not sure. I love my boys both dearly and more than anything in this world.

I often think back on what happened to me, sometimes crying. I can remember a point when I couldn't even look my abuser in his eyes even in my thoughts. Now, with a God sent strength, when I see 'him' in passing, I can say, "Hey, how are you?" Only God can fix a heart that allows you to be kind to your 'enemy'. I have overcome this. It doesn't have a choke hold on my life. I am greater than it. I have grown from a little girl who has the weight of the world on her shoulders into a woman that juggles with ease a new world in which she is not afraid.

Sincerely,

    Tarnished & Tainted

## THE BABY SITTERS

My father called me into the room to discuss the incident that could have traumatized my three year old daughter (Veronica) had I not listened to her. I had left Veronica and my oldest son Kevin in the care of a male friend who happened to be a minister of the church I attended. (The minister's niece and nephews also resided in the home.) An emergency situation had warranted me to attend to my youngest son, Mark, who had been admitted into the hospital for a week. I stayed with Mark day and night until I could take him home, as he had nearly died from dehydration and a bacterial infection brought on by Chicken Pox. Mark was almost 2 years old at the time, and he was too frightened for me to leave him.

I had always taught my children at a very young age, that if anyone touched their privates, (I used anatomical names at the time) to say "No!" and to tell me immediately. The day Mark was discharged from the hospital; I went to pick Veronica and Kevin up from the Minister's home. Everything seemed normal. The minister told me everything went well and my children were well behaved and had a great time. I expressed my gratefulness for the caring of my children, as I was a single mother, and did not have anyone else to help me. With that, I took my children home.

That evening, I gave my daughter a bath and as I was drying her off, she pointed to her private, and told me that the minister touched her Vagina. I asked her what she said, as I was totally shocked by her words. She said, "Charles touched my vagina." I began to ask her questions, "How did he touch your vagina?" "Show me where he touched you." With that she put her hand to her vagina and rubbed. I confirmed with Veronica a few times to ensure the accuracy of the incident, as I knew that a three year old would not just make anything up.

Charles had given Veronica baths in those seven days she was at his home. After her bath, he would lay out a towel on the bed. At the time, my daughter was recovering from Chicken Pox as well, and he would put cream on her privates, and he took advantage of that and rubbed her Vagina improperly as I had not told him to put any cream on her private area.

After making a report to the Child Protection Services, I discovered that Charles had two prior reported accusations that had not been taken to trial. So here I am talking to my father and he is telling me that as a responsible parent, I should have taken extra precautions and protected Veronica. Those words stung my heart as it felt as though I was being slapped in the face. I looked at my dad and yelled, "Well! How can you say that to me when you didn't protect me!!! I am a good parent!! How can you say that to me, when you let someone molest me?" My father's face dropped, as he had no idea what I was talking about. I didn't even know that these feelings were deep inside of me, and that I held on to them for at least 20 years.

My parents were community and civic leaders and went to many events at night in the course of my upbringing. My parents would leave my brother who was a few years older with neighborhood teenagers or college students while they went out on the town. I am pretty sure my parents didn't worry about anything strange happening to us, as the babysitters came from "good" homes.

When I was five years old, I had a one-time male babysitter (Jim) that I think was in his twenties. Jim was a next door neighbor. He had younger siblings that he had to watch on a regular basis. My brother and I were in our pajamas the evening that Jim came to watch us. We were watching television, which was a rare occasion in our household. As we were watching television, Jim got off the couch and left the room. A few minutes or so, I hear him call my name. I head towards his voice, and find Jim sitting in my room on my bed. He tells me to close the door. I do. I then noticed that his pants were down and he is touching himself and this white stuff is coming from his private. I am not aware of what he is doing, and I think it really strange. He tells me to touch it. I tell him "No!" He grabs my hand

and tries to make me touch his penis, but I keep my hand clenched in a fist. Right when he is doing that, my brother knocks on the bedroom door. He opens the door and sees what is going on and tells me that he is going to tell mom and dad. I didn't know what I did wrong. I didn't even know why all of this was happening. My brother and I never talked about this incident, and Jim was never seen at our house again.

Another incident happened with another male babysitter (Richard) that only came over one time. I was probably about six at the time, and I was getting ready for bed. Richard pushed his way in my room. I had nothing on. He picked me up and carried me in the living room, spread eagle, and chased my brother around the room with my private showing. I remember my brother laughing and trying to get away. It was a very awkward and uncomfortable situation. Nothing was said after this strange occurrence, but Richard told my parents that he was not going to babysit us again because I was a strange little girl. "Wow is all I could say." Richard must have had a reason, and it seemed to me he was trying to protect himself.

After revealing these stories to my father, he felt very sad that these things had happened to me. At that moment, he realized that the protection of our children must come in forms of communication and teaching our children how to say, "No!" We must let them know that it is important to not be afraid and they must tell someone if they are ever violated.

Sincerely,

Naïve and Unaware

## JUST A THOUGHT

I think deep down when a woman thinks back on the assault of child sexual abuse there is a part of her that will always wonder, was it my fault? The physical aspect is bad but what's worse is the mental factor. Psychologically manipulated, the abuser not only looks to take innocence but he seeks to control the mind. Rape is the ultimate struggle for power.

## READY OR NOT

There are many excuses as to why we wait to disclose the abuse. Fear of retaliation from the abuser, always waiting for the right time that never seems to come, uncertain of how others will react, feeling that somehow the abuse was our fault…Personally, as with the stories I've gathered, there is a longing for security; the reassurance that we, not our abusers, are in control. The "he can't hurt me now" syndrome usually does not manifest itself until mental security is established, which we automatically assume accompanies age. Women in their late 20's to mid-30 were trending amongst those that came forward. These women for the most part have come to a comfortable resting place in their lives. Those younger were not as thorough in detail and there was still a great deal of emotional confusion. The oldest to share her story (50 + years young) presented much discomfort as she had never told another. The sense of shame was fresh in her words, old wounds that have yet to heal, ladened shoulders weary from the secret they've upheld. The healing process is an essential part of our lives. To transition from Victim to Survivor is a beautiful thing! But first we must acknowledge the hurt done and accept that we in no way are to blame. It's time we speak up! For ourselves, for our daughters, for our daughter's daughters! Who's ready?

## 1x A VICTIM

Brief details. Sheltered child. Raised by a now forgiven mother. Back then cheated on by her husband and unhappy, she began taking her anger out on her daughter. Mother threatened to "beat your ass if you let somebody play in your pocketbook," yet takes daughter to her older cousin's house to be babysat and (unknown to mother) MOLESTED.

I wanted to tell her, but I was afraid because she said (with a passion) that she would beat my ass. Picked on at school, abused at Auntie's house and spending too much time alone… but my mother was busy, absorbed in my Father and his itinerary, she didn't notice anything. I was 10. I can remember this one time going on a trip with the family; mother, aunt, grandmother, uncles, and siblings (mine and his). We're in the van and 'he' starts feeling me up right there!!! That was the last straw because I knew that I was going to get my ass whipped for sure if he was to get caught by my mother. Thing is, I thought that they would have blamed me and not him. I was 12 ½. I get so pissed at life sometimes because bless her heart, my mother, my parents… I feel 'they' held me back. My cousin has apologized and I have since forgiven him.

Sincerely,

Who Would Have Believed Me

## x2

Future encounters of rape are highly likely. The 1x victim's disposition leaves fragile minds in a state of shock. Put in a situation the body panics, the mouth does not say "yes", but the mind is too afraid to say "no"…

- Many years later I was raped by a soldier. The stereotype that they have pussy thrown at them so why would they have to take it, precedes them. I knew no one would believe me. I remained silent.

-It was like deja vu. It was just something about the way my mother's then boyfriend looked at me. The same hungry look I had interpreted as 'love' in my Daddy's eyes. So instead of being hurt, I told myself that I wanted to feel his tongue licking me, thrusting in and out of me, sucking me. It was better than being raped… again. This time I was in control? It was the summer of 1993, I was 13.

## 4 DECADES HAVE PASSED

Remembering the old. Where do I start and finish? As a young girl not knowing truth and trusting the men around me, thinking they love me and want the best for me. That is where I start my story. A family affair that goes on in every family, but a secret you keep to yourself instead of telling and hurting others around you. A secret you keep to yourself because, who will believe you. Understand, my first encounter was when I was 11, my body and mind was changing. Afterwards, I felt that they [all men] were dogs, I understand this feeling now, but when I was younger I didn't. They made me feel it was my fault, like I had asked for it and this was the way to become a woman. I remember seeing my cousin being abused by her stepfather and I finally understood what was going on around me. I thought, this is life, and went on. The abusers made it a 'reward' event, small gifts and more love given. At that time, it was only touching me, but when I turned thirteen my life was turned into a world of strange events. As a young girl I developed very early and men started to notice. The men I trusted took all my trust away. I knew the pain would never leave. I felt less than I was worth. Taken by a man, I knew that a man could not give me that feeling of self-worth back. Still, life must go on with those around you, but I knew that what was done was sick and would never be forgotten. As the years went by and I matured, I began to understand what it was I wanted from a relationship, but I had to throw those old feeling of hurt in the trash where they belonged. This has helped me deal with life. It has helped me become the strong woman I am today. But old hurts don't die so easily. Four decades later my past affects me, affects those around me, my own family. I hold back my feelings. Touch and smell have been affected by child sexual abuse. I am sharing my story because my secret can help someone else. The pain stops for you NOW! But first you must love yourself. Part of my healing has been in having God in my life and looking for answers as to why this happened to me. We live in a world of sin. Understanding this has set me free, but I still remember and remembering keeps us and future generations safe. Don't forget.

Sincerely,

This shared in Remembrance

## SHORT TERM/LONG TERM: BODY & PSYCHE

Some short term effects include: Anti-social behavior, internal lacerations, vaginitis, sexual confusion, morbid thoughts, denial, difficulty sleeping, self-blame, low self-esteem, shame, anger, withdrawal, confusion, headaches, severed friendships, an overall feeling of being lost, short term memory loss...

Some long term effects include: Post traumatic stress disorder (PTSD), nightmares, disassociation, difficulty relating to others except on sexual terms, seductiveness, promiscuity, scar tissue, reoccurring vaginitis, depression, damage to the hippocampus, abdominal complaint, poor coping and decision making skills, inability to orgasm, difficulty in relationships, trust issues, repressed memory…

The memory is a funny thing, often blocking out that which is too hard to deal with or too difficult to understand. In the mind of the victim, pretty portraits lay in the wake of the holes nails have left behind. The victim 'forgets' the incidence just as quickly as it happens or the memory fades over time. This is our subconscious way of "moving on."

## THE TIME IS NOW

Within these pages we hurt, we share, we cry, we offer support, we acknowledge, we remember, we begin to heal. The time is now. Why wait until tomorrow? We already know the chances of child sexual abuse being a one-time event is highly unlikely (see RECIDIVISM). So if not you, then another innocent little girl awaits the same fate! Why wait? The time is now! It's time we get mad and get even. There is a score to settle. We owe it to ourselves. We owe it to every little girl in the world. We owe it to the little girl that still lives in each of us. She is not dead. She is simply waiting for the storm to subside. She is waiting for you to decide to be a victim no more. To be a Survivor takes Courage, Faith, and a Determination that is both fierce and feared. Within these pages we leave old hurts behind. The damage has been done, now the Dawn of a new day is upon us. Speak up for you or for someone else. It only takes 120 seconds... 2 minutes! In the amount of time it takes to read the daily headline, solve a simple riddle, brush your teeth, or give a meaningful hug, another woman has been raped. From 2000-2005, 59% of rapes were not reported to law enforcement (rainn.org 2008-01-01). It's time we speak up and speak out. It's time we end the cycle and break the chain. It's time we SURVIVE.

ANGEL EYES FOUNDATION CHALLENGE:

## PREPARE THE BATTLEFIELD & ENCOURAGE SELF-ESTEEM

The low self-esteem seen in girls does not disappear with maturity; girls with low self-esteem often grow to be women with low self-esteem. Low levels of self-esteem are linked to increased rates of depression, substance abuse, suicide and eating disorders in both adolescents and adults (How Schools Shortchange Girls, 1992; Melpomene Institute, 1996).

Children, who are confident, are more aware of their own voices. This certainty assures them of their right to say no. This strength discourages potential child sexual abuse. As a parent, I'm aware that we yearn for compliant children. But a child that is afraid to question authority could possibly be a child that becomes the target of a predator. When we encourage self-esteem in our children we boost the awareness of their own personal strength. What perpetrator would wisely target a child that is confident, sure, and unafraid to say 'no'? This very child is more likely to disclose any abuse. A healthy and positive self-esteem may very well be your child's most important weapon against child sexual abuse.

A few signs of low self-esteem:

- Withdrawn, fear of interaction
- Not many, if any friends
- Sad, depressed
- Negative self-image

- Loner syndrome, anti-social

What can we as Parents & Guardians do to Prepare the Battlefield?

- Replace negative thoughts with positive ones
- Celebrate achievements
- Teach realistic goal setting
- Stress the importance of trusting your own feelings
- Acknowledge and reward effort
- Be a positive role model, one your child admires and trusts
- Give positive feedback, especially after an upset
- Provide a safe, loving, and nurturing environment
- Allow decision making opportunities
- Encourage your child to speak his or her mind

Be mindful of your own words. Don't put them down, build them up!

*On a personal note. Self-esteem for girls is not just about how we look, it's about how we feel about how we look as well. Do not allow the mirror or peer pressure or the media to become your daughter's nemesis, instead become her bestfriend and tell her daily how beautiful she is and that beauty radiates from within*

## EXPOSE... EDUCATE... EMANCIPATE... ENCOURAGE... EMPOWER

Expose our daughters to the awareness of this threat, expose our own feelings about child sexual abuse, and expose the truths that surround this crime.

Educate our daughters; teach them 'Good Touch/Bad Touch. Allow the education to grow as they mature and allow the education to continue. Educate yourself so that we will recognize the warning signs. Education in all things is key.

Emancipate our own discomforts involving 'sex talk', emancipate our children, especially our daughters to speak confidently in their own voices. Emancipate them from the old ways of "Children should be seen, not heard." Emancipate them of uncomfortable situations, never forcing hello's to strangers or hugs to relatives. Emancipate them to feel free.

Encourage our daughters to express their thoughts, to share their feelings. Encourage them to seek 'help' when faced with any threatening situation.

Empower our daughters with the knowledge to be safe, the strength to fight back, and the courage to speak up. Empower them with a reassurance that child sexual abuse is never their fault.

# THE CYCLE OF PROTECTION

Prevent child sexual abuse by Protecting.

Protect by Providing knowledge & safety.

And if this should fail…

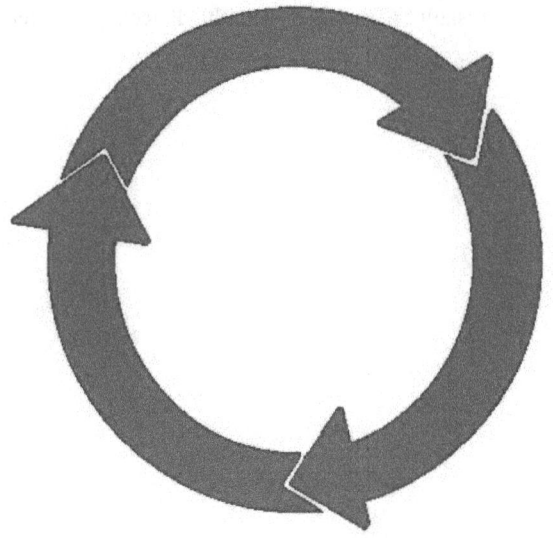

Promise to 'hear' the voice when it tells.

Promise to Prevent the hurt from happening again.

Provide law enforcement with allegations and

seek proper medical and psychological help.

Promise to be there NO MATTER WHAT.

# DECLARATIONS

April 8, 2009, President Barack Obama officially declared April as National Sexual Assault Awareness Month.

Peace over Violence day, a rape prevention education campaign started a movement in 1999, Denim Day which embodies the truths that the clothes we wear, even "very tight jeans" cannot prevent nor provoke sexual abuse "There is no excuse and never an invitation to rape." The number of participants is growing rapidly. April 27th, 2011 was my first observance. Call to Action: I say we vote this an official observance, as a part of National Sexual Assault Awareness Month. Placed on calendars and nationally observed, so we don't forget. RAPE IS REAL!

*DENIM DAY 2012 WILL BE OBSERVED ON APRIL 25TH*

Check the site for future dates!

http://denimdayinla.org

# AFTERWORD

In the midst of writing this book, my teenage son came to look over my shoulders to 'see' what his mother was working on. In a panic, I turned pages over and covered what I felt to be 'private' in an attempt to protect him. But I realized in an instance the harm I had done in that single act and sought to correct it. My teenage son, whose eyes are becoming more aware of the female form, who's body is reacting on a chemical level, who on occasion speaks of the fairer sex. I knew it was time for the talk. Not just any ol' sex talk where you tell em' abstinence is best, but if you must, use a condom for protection. No this was the 'Be mindful and respectful in every way" talk. When a girl says no, even in a laughing manner, back off. Because he is my oldest child and he and I have a very open relationship, I felt that I could disclose to him my own abuse. He was shocked but there was a sense of appreciation. His mother's spirit had been beaten, but it was far from broken. That brought me out of my comfort zone and reminded me to do the once routine Q & A with my daughters. The "has anyone made you feel icky… touch your vagina or any other private part… what do you do if someone touches you in a bad way or make you do something that is wrong… who else besides those in the home can you speak to if you're ever hurt… do you know that mom will love you no matter what?" So many questions, so many answers… but answers just the same. Life is not always nice. There's no need in me hiding in my office typing romance novels all day and reading fairytales at night in an attempt to shelter my children. Then it dawned on me. The best protection I can provide is to place in their hands the power for them to protect themselves. I will be encouraging this strength daily. Child sexual abuse ends here! Knowledge is key. Awareness is a must. Every voice shall be heard!

# BIBLIOGRAPHY & RESOURCES

www.rainn.org

1-800-656-HOPE (4673) RAINN

http://denimdayusa.org

www.wikepedia.org

http://dictionary.reference.com

www.meganslaw.ca.gov

www.siawso.org

http://uslegal.com

http://en.cyberdodo.com

http://aacap.org

American Academy of Child & Adolescent Psychiatry

www.medicinenet.com

www.now.org

www.ifsha.org

www.yellodyno.com

www.amnestyusa.org

http://www.cdcfoundation.org/what/program/together-girls

Center for Disease Control

www.darkness2light.org

http://www.troubledwith.com/AbuseandAddiction/SexualAbuse.cfm

http://www.allaboutcounseling.com/

http://neuro.psychiatryonline.org

http://news.bbc.co.uk

Each bibliography listed serves as a great resource

## Angel Eyes Foundation; Social Advocacy Organization

Child sexual abuse is real but it is not incurable. It is AEF's mission to create awareness, provide information and educate our communities. We can never be too cautious with our children; especially our daughters... but we can't hold their hands every second of every day. My purpose and goal is to teach parents to equip their children with those skills that can possibly protect their innocence. For example: Talking. Do you know how hard it is to hurt a child that has an openly verbal communication with a trusting parent or other adult? Can you imagine this very child feeling more secure to tell you anything? This is the brunt of AEF. To raise that awareness. To let the world know, "Hey, I'm here, I'm learning how to protect my children, I'm being educated and the awareness is raised." Potential child sexual abusers 'know' an easy target. Let's take the bull's eye off of the face of every child. Thank you!!

Angel Eyes Foundation is a 501 (c) 3 Non-profit organization.

P O Box 161965

Atlanta Georgia 30321

Founded by Katandra Shanel Jackson.

Website: http://angeleyesfoundation.blogspot.com

Twitter: @aef_forgetmenot

Facebook: facebook.com/AngelEyesFoundation501c3

Email: aef@freedomink365.com

# AUTHOR BIO

Katandra Shanel Jackson is the proud Chief Everything Officer at FreedomInk Publishing! Throughout her day, she dons many hats, steps into many roles, and oversees the production of a plethora of simultaneous projects. To date, FreedomInk has published 4 books, Angel Eyes: A Collective Memoir of Child Sexual Abuse, being one of those titles. This book is very dear to Katandra, as she herself has had to come to terms that what is done is done. Katandra is a bride to be, daughter, aunt, niece, friend, and mother of 3. She has penned a book entitled, The Diary of A Bride To Be Book 1: A Reason, A Season or A Lifetime. At current, The Diary of A Bride To Be Book 2: The Return of Spring is being composed. The Bride Diaries will be revised and released via FreedomInk Publishing, summer 2012.

In addition to FreedomInk, Katandra is the Founder of The Angel Eyes Foundation. The purpose in this social advocacy platform is to raise and promote awareness on the dangers of child sexual abuse, online and in the community. The Author/Publisher resides in Atlanta Georgia, with her fiancé' and their three children. She too, is the SURVIVOR…

Are you or anyone you know the survivor of child sexual abuse? Have you found the courage to come forward? Have you discovered an outlet to help you cope? Please join those that wish to remain silent no more. The dragon is defeated by the words of your testimony. We each have a story to tell! Pick up the pen and begin…

Write to your heart's content. Until fingers bleed and tears have retreated. Write until you've come completely undone and the only thing left to do is move on.

Write!

Father, Buddha, Allah, all the Powers that be; thank you for the serenity, courage and wisdom to complete 'Angel Eyes: A Collective Memoir of Child Sexual Abuse'! I pray that it speaks in the darkness and sheds light on the truth. With unknowing heart, and denying senses…

Open your heart and listen. ~KSJ

www.ingramcontent.com/pod-product-compliance
Lightning Source LLC
Chambersburg PA
CBHW071407160426
42813CB00084B/725